Animal World
THE PENGUIN

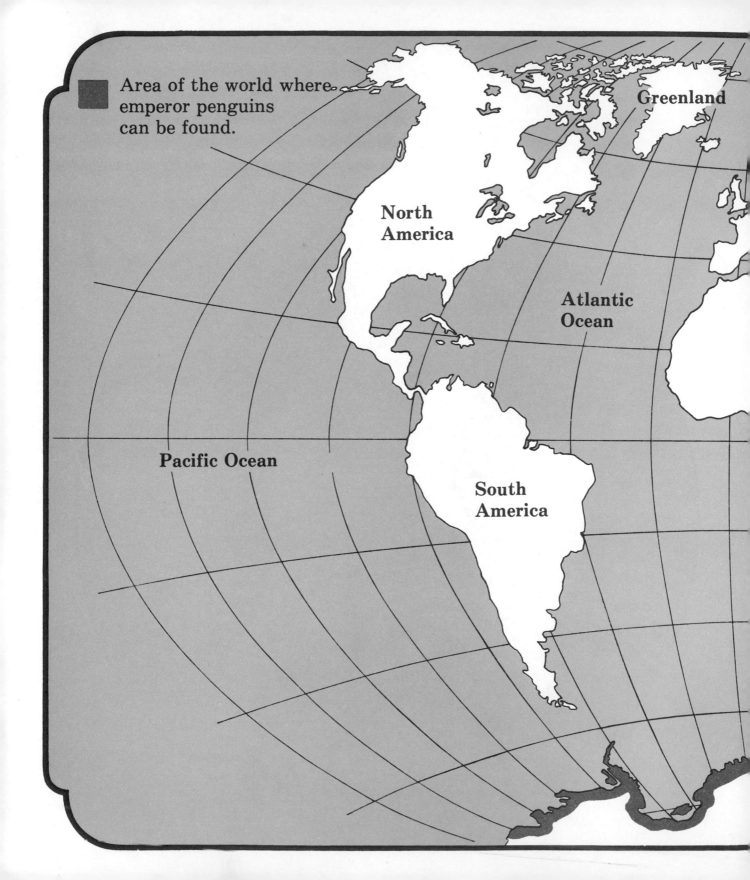

Area of the world where emperor penguins can be found.

Greenland

North America

Atlantic Ocean

Pacific Ocean

South America

Published by Watermill Press, Mahwah, New Jersey.
Copyright © 1983 by The Rourke Enterprises, Inc. All copyrights reserved. No part of this book may be reproduced in any form without written permission from the publisher. Printed in the United States of America.

Library of Congress Cataloging in Publication Data

Dalmais, Anne-Marie, 1954-
  The penguin.

  (Animal world)
  Translation of: Le manchot.
  Reprint. Originally published: London : Macdonald
Educational, 1979.
  Summary: Text and illustrations introduce the natural environment, physical characteristics, and habits of the emperor penguin.
  1. Emperor penguin — Juvenile literature.   [1. Emperor] penguin.   2. Penguins]   I. Weaver, Norman, ill.
II. Title.   III. Series.
QL696.S473D3413   1984   598.4'41   83-9784
ISBN 0-86592-854-1

Animal World
THE PENGUIN

illustrated by
Norman Weaver

Watermill Press
Mahwah, New Jersey

On the ice of Antarctica

A big mass of ice sparkles in the summer sun. It is floating near the coast of the Antarctic continent. This continent is in the Southern Hemisphere. It is as large as Europe but no one lives on it. The climate is too harsh. In winter the temperature falls to minus 160 °F. Even in summer it does not rise higher than 32 °F.

The landscape is partly mountains of rock. Some of them are 19,000 feet high. There are also vast plains and steep cliffs. Everything is covered with a thick layer of ice that never melts. It is difficult to reach this frozen continent because there are gigantic icebergs in the way, as well as sheets of ice that are carried along by the currents.

The sheets of ice are where the emperor penguins live for part of the year. These large birds cannot fly. They have small wings but they use them for swimming. Look at the group in the picture. You can tell they are penguins from a long way off because they stand up so straight.

A pair of penguins

Here is a pair of emperor penguins, one male and the
other female. You can see that they are very alike. They
have the same long, pointed beaks, black on top and
orange underneath. They both have strong, rounded
bodies and their narrow stiff wings are the same. So is
their thick black and white plumage. Their legs are
short and black and have webbed feet. The male is a
little bigger than the female.

Penguins look clumsy when they walk. When they see
the ground sloping down in front of them, they throw
themselves flat on their bellies and slide along as if they
were tobogganing.

In the water

Penguins are happiest when they are in the water. They are splendid swimmers. They can compete with such champions as seals and porpoises, leaping gracefully out of the water and diving deep. They push themselves forward with their wings and steer with their feet. They can reach a speed of 25 miles per hour.

Here you see the male coming to the surface, while the female leaps into the air and lands on the ice.

Penguins find all their food in the sea. They eat fish and squid, but they like shrimps best of all.

Enemies of the penguin

Penguins have few natural enemies. The only animals in the sea that can swim fast enough to attack them are killer whales and leopard seals.

On the left of the picture you can see a leopard seal lifting its head above the drifting ice. This creature belongs to the seal family. It is fierce, greedy and a very fast, agile swimmer. When it sees a penguin, it swims in a circle around it. The penguin cannot escape from the circle because it cannot fly. When it is exhausted, the leopard seal pounces on it.

The killer whale on the right is the largest and fiercest member of the dolphin family. It goes after penguins and slashes them with its sharp teeth.

On land

At the beginning of autumn the penguins leave the floating ice and swim ashore. Thousands of them gather there.

Every year the penguins come back to the same places to lay their eggs. But once they leave the sea, they have to do without food because there is none on land for them. For weeks they eat nothing. They live on the fat that is stored in their bodies.

The eggs are laid

Now it is time for the penguins to mate. Males and females do a dance which is called a mating display. Two months later, the females lay their eggs. Each female lays a single white egg weighing about 15 ounces. Then she goes back to the sea to feed. She leaves the male to hatch the egg.

The male balances the egg on his feet and keeps it warm under a fold of the skin on his belly. It is very cold now and the males need protection from the blizzards. They all huddle together taking turns to stand in the sheltered places in the middle of the group.

The penguin chicks

The eggs hatch two months later. At the same time the females return from the sea and take over for the males. Now it is the fathers' turn to go in search of food, which they so badly need. They have lost nearly 33 pounds in weight.

While the fathers are away, the mothers look after the chicks. Each baby penguin stays hidden in its mother's plumage for another 2 to 3 weeks. The chicks are funny to look at with their light grey downy feathers. Their mothers feed them on juices and fats produced by their own digestive tubes.

Watching over the young

When the fathers have eaten enough to regain their full weight, they come back to help look after the chicks. The young penguins grow up in large groups. Hundreds of them are gathered together and are watched over by the adult penguins. They are now old enough to eat fish. The parents catch the fish in the sea and bring them back in their crops, which are pouches below their gullets for storing food. Then they put the fish into the infants' beaks. This goes on for three months. Soon the ice begins to crack and the parents do not have so far to go in search of fish for their young.

Back to the sea

At last, summer comes to Antarctica. The penguins lose their old feathers and grow new ones. This is called molting. With their new plumage, all the birds return to the sea. The young live on their own now, swimming and diving happily in the ice cold waters of the Antarctic Ocean.

SOME INTERESTING FACTS ABOUT PENGUINS

Species:

Penguins belong to the scientific family of Spheniscidae. They have been around for 50 million years. The first penguins lived in the Antarctic, New Zealand and South America. The biggest fossil penguin ever discovered stood 5 feet 8 inches tall. No modern penguin is that tall.

Penguins are birds. However, they differ from other birds in two respects: one, their wings are really flippers and two, they do not fly.

There are 17 species of penguins. Two of them live in the Antarctic. The rest are scattered throughout the Southern Hemisphere. There are no penguins in the Northern Hemisphere.

Description:

The word *penguin* is Welsh. It means "whitehead." Penguins have a white front and a black back. They look like they are wearing tuxedos.

Penguins are flightless birds that "fly" through the water. They are great swimmers. They live in water and come on land only to breed and raise their young.

Their bodies are well designed for swimming. Their feathers are so small and tightly packed that they look like scales. Because of this, they can move through the water sleekly. Feathers also provide insulation. Penguins swim in very cold water. Their feet are used for steering. Powerful flippers provide propulsion. Those flippers enable them to swim with great strength. Sometimes a penguin will surface so forcefully that it will soar through the air. On land, the flippers are used for fighting. Penguins look comical when they walk. They have a waddle. Sometimes they flop on their bellies and slide.

In 1975 an American scientist named Kooyman studied the diving habits of penguins. He found that they can dive much deeper than people imagined. They go to depths of 800 feet and can stay down for 18 minutes.

The largest penguin is the emperor penguin. An adult stands 4 feet tall and weighs about 60 pounds. It lives in the Antarctic. Some people think that it is the most beautiful of all penguins. It has a purple bill and its "bib" is golden and shiny.

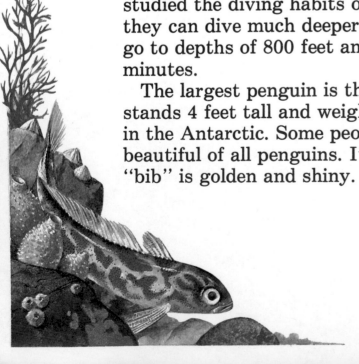

The macaroni penguin is not well known. It lives in the sub-Antarctic and the islands in the cold regions of all three oceans. It is very different in appearance from the emperor. At 2 feet tall and weighing only about 10 pounds, it is one of the smaller penguins. It has long, bright, yellow plumes growing from the top of its head. It looks like it is wearing a crown.

The Galapagos penguin is very rare. There are only about 4,000 of these in the world. It lives on the Galapagos Islands. It is the only penguin to live so near the equator. It likes to live close to the warm sea waters, in caves or cliffs.

The rockhopper penguin is named for its habit of jumping or hopping from rock to rock while holding its feet together. It was savagely massacred in the millions by men who wanted its oil.

Family Life:

Males and females live apart, except during the breeding season. Most penguins have similar mating habits. The breeding season begins on October and extends into the six-month-long polar night.

Both males and females will spend the months prior to October swimming and fishing. They want to eat as much as possible at this time. They will not be able to eat later.

In October, the males will climb on shore and head for the breeding grounds. These are called "rookeries." All penguins have established rookeries that they go to year after year. The male will go to the nest and wait for the female to arrive. When she gets there, they greet each other. This is done with neck stretches and flipper waves. This is called the "mutual display." It is part of their ritual.

In November, the female lays one egg. Some penguins, like the Adelie, lay two. She then goes back to the sea to feed. Unlike some fathers, the male penguin plays a vital role in the birth of his young. If the egg were left alone at this point, it would surely freeze. The father incubates the egg by carrying it on his large feet. His body temperature keeps it warm. To keep from freezing himself, he gathers in a huddle with all the other fathers. It is a long vigil. The temperatures can reach 70 degrees below zero, and it is always dark. In some species the female returns to incubate the egg. This is called the "changing of the guard." They greet each other with excited "mutual displays." The male quickly goes off to sea. He has not eaten in about 6 weeks.

The incubation period is about 40 days. One exception, the king penguin, takes as long as 54 days. The baby weighs about 11 ounces and is covered with gray down. Since there is nothing for it to eat in this frozen place, the parents must feed their babies in a strange manner. They take turns going to sea and collecting fish in their bills. They do not swallow the fish. They return to the nest and allow the baby to pick the fish out of their bills. This is the only food the baby has.

It is now January. It is still dark and very cold. All the babies huddle together as their fathers did. This huddle is called a "creche." Soon the ice will begin to break up and parents and young will head for the open sea.

Penguins are noisy, social creatures. They will gladly take care of each other's young. Most penguins are mature at 4 years of age. They live between 25 and 30 years.

Conservation:

Penguins love to be in the water. They spend most of their time there. If a hunter is after them, he will go to their breeding grounds. Because penguins always return to the same rookery every year, he knows where to find them. Penguins do not move quickly on land, so they are nearly helpless. Some penguins, like the rockhopper, have valuable stores of oil. For this reason they were preyed on and killed in the millions.

Penguin chicks are in danger from the leopard seal. Leopard seals will wait just under the ice. They pounce on young penguins just as they are about to take their first swim.

Men cannot do much about the threat of leopard seals, but they can control human hunters. The people of 11 nations of the Southern Hemisphere have banded together to protect the penguin. Their rookeries are now protected by international law. Many of them are bird sanctuaries.